Muck & Magic

Start your own natural garden with colourful, simple projects

Jo Readman

with illustrations by Polly Pinder

Henry Doubleday Research Association/Search Press

Contents

About this book

This book gives lots of tips and practical advice on how to grow plants organically. Organic gardening is fun. It is not just about growing plants without chemicals, but about working with nature and getting the creatures in the garden to help you. Ask at home, or at school, if you can have a small plot of land where you can grow your plants. When you have decided what to grow, draw a plan of your plot to make sure that you can fit it all in. Do not worry if you cannot get hold of any ground, as a lot of the activities shown in this book can be carried out in pots, either in your back-yard or on a sunny window-sill.

Look out for the ladybird throughout the book and try to answer her questions. (You will find the answers on page 45.)

635 REA

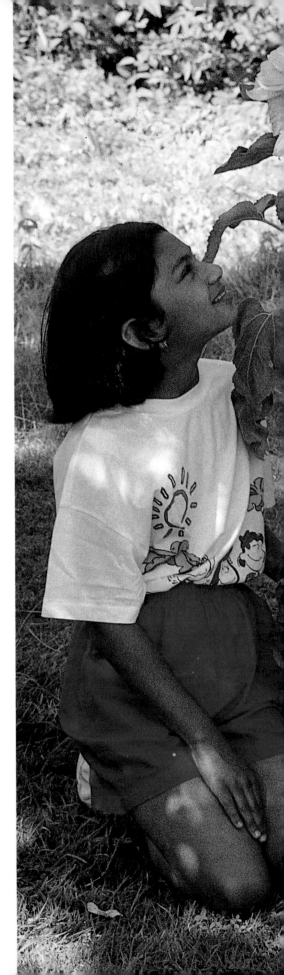

The Author and Publishers would like to thank Sareena, Jonathan, Kelly, Ben, Lizzie, Paul, Emily, Anish, Daniel, Matthew, and Nikki for posing so patiently for the photographs. The Author would also like to thank all the children at High Littleton Primary School who helped her to decide upon the content of the book. The book is dedicated to Jake and Charlie.

First published in Great Britain 1993 by Search Press Ltd., Wellwood, North Farm Road, Tunbridge Wells, Kent TN2 3DR, in association with The Henry Doubleday Research Association, National Centre for Organic Gardening, Ryton-on-Dunsmore, Coventry CV8 3LG. Text copyright © 1993 Henry Doubleday Research Association. Illustrations, photographs, and design copyright © 1993 Search Press Ltd.

This book covers parts of the science module of the National Curriculum up to level 5, including attainment targets 1 and 2 (namely, scientific investigation, and life and living processes).

ISBN 0 85532 757 X

Made and printed in Spain by A. G. Elkar, S. Coop. 48012 Bilbao

What is organic gardening?

Organic means something that is or was once alive. Organic gardens are a part of nature, filled with lots of different plants and garden wildlife. Organic gardeners try to understand and work with nature to help the garden grow. They do not use chemical fertilizers to feed plants or use chemical sprays to kill pests.

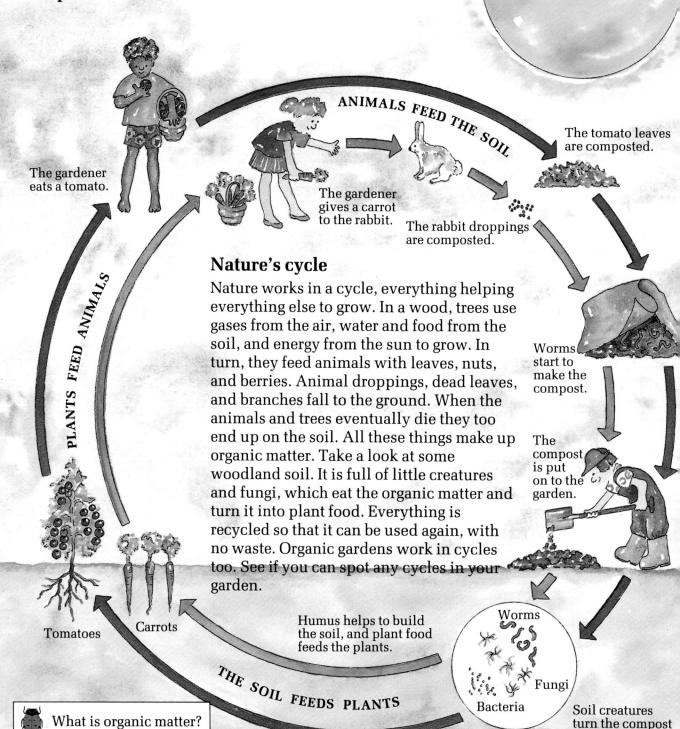

THE SUN HELPS PLANTS TO G

ANIMALS FEED THE SOIL

The tomato leaves are composted.

The gardener eats a tomato.

The gardener gives a carrot to the rabbit.

The rabbit droppings are composted.

Worms start to make the compost.

The compost is put on to the garden.

PLANTS FEED ANIMALS

Nature's cycle

Nature works in a cycle, everything helping everything else to grow. In a wood, trees use gases from the air, water and food from the soil, and energy from the sun to grow. In turn, they feed animals with leaves, nuts, and berries. Animal droppings, dead leaves, and branches fall to the ground. When the animals and trees eventually die they too end up on the soil. All these things make up organic matter. Take a look at some woodland soil. It is full of little creatures and fungi, which eat the organic matter and turn it into plant food. Everything is recycled so that it can be used again, with no waste. Organic gardens work in cycles too. See if you can spot any cycles in your garden.

Humus helps to build the soil, and plant food feeds the plants.

Tomatoes

Carrots

Worms

Fungi

Bacteria

THE SOIL FEEDS PLANTS

Soil creatures turn the compost into plant food and humus.

What is organic matter?

4

How does the soil work?

The soil is the most important part of the garden.

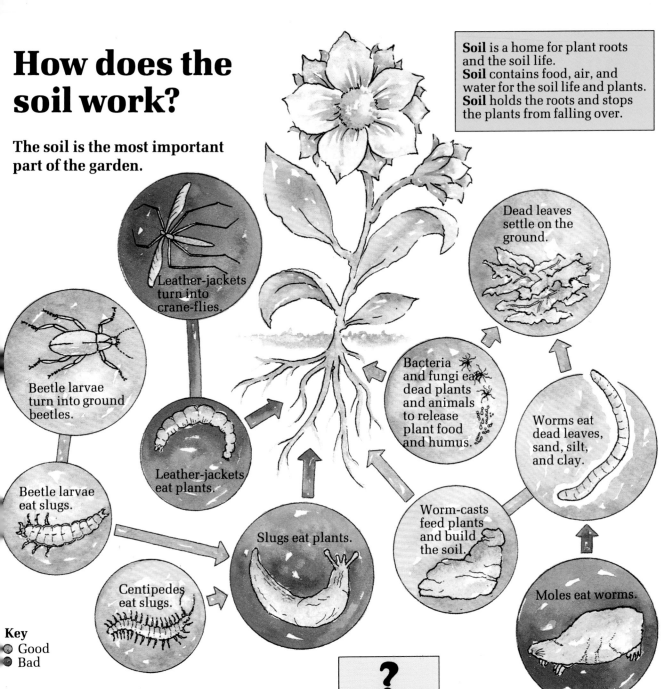

Leather-jackets turn into crane-flies.

Beetle larvae turn into ground beetles.

Leather-jackets eat plants.

Beetle larvae eat slugs.

Dead leaves settle on the ground.

Bacteria and fungi eat dead plants and animals to release plant food and humus.

Worms eat dead leaves, sand, silt, and clay.

Slugs eat plants.

Worm-casts feed plants and build the soil.

Centipedes eat slugs.

Moles eat worms.

Key
◐ Good
◑ Bad

Examining the soil

Find a patch of soil where you can dig a large hole. Dig out the soil and take a look at it. Look, too, at the sides of the hole.

The soil life likes to live near the top of the soil, in the topsoil. Try not to mix the topsoil and the subsoil, as the creatures do not like having their house turned upside-down.

?

What colour is the surface of the soil?
The darker the colour the more organic matter the soil usually contains.

?

Do the top few centimetres of the soil contain any roots, creatures, or worm channels?
This is the topsoil where all the life is. The more worms the better, and the deeper this soil the better.

?

What does the soil smell like?
Helpful soil creatures make the soil smell sweet. If there is too much water and not enough air, then it will smell of bad eggs.

?

Does the soil change colour further down?
Under the topsoil is the subsoil. This is a different colour and has less soil life in it.

 Why smell the soil?

What is in the soil?

You can tell what type of soil you have just by picking up a handful, feeling it, and moulding it.

Moulding sandy soil into a ball.

Moulding clay soil into a sausage shape.

Minerals

Soil contains ground-up rocks called minerals.

Sandy soil has big particles and feels gritty. It can be moulded into a ball, but it crumbles if you try to make a sausage shape out of it. It is easy to dig and warms up quickly in the spring. It does not contain much plant food, and water drains out of it quickly, rather like it does from the sand on a beach.

Clay soil has very small particles and feels sticky. It can be moulded into a sausage shape which may even be bent into a ring. It holds on to lots of plant food and water. It is difficult to dig, setting like concrete when dry and sticking to your spade and boots when wet.

Luckily, soils usually have a mixture of sand and clay. Also, good old organic matter helps to cure many of the problems.

Organic matter

This is a very important part of the soil and is the key to healthy soil. It is turned into plant food and humus (a black, jelly-like substance), and it helps to hold the soil together. It makes clays less sticky, and it helps sandy soils to hold on to their food and water.

Air

Put some soil into a glass of water. Can you see the air bubbles coming out? This air lets roots and soil creatures breathe. When you water the soil the stale air is pushed out and when the water drains away fresh air is sucked in.

Water

Weigh a handful of soil and ask an adult to put it in the oven for twenty minutes. Then, weigh it

again. The difference in weight is due to the water in the soil, which has evaporated in the heat of the oven.

 What is the key to healthy soil?

6

Who lives in the soil?

Plant roots and many small creatures live in the soil. Like humans, they need air, food, water, and a little bit of space. They live in 'rooms' between crumbs of soil. The crumbs are stuck together by the soil life, using humus and glues just like we use cement.

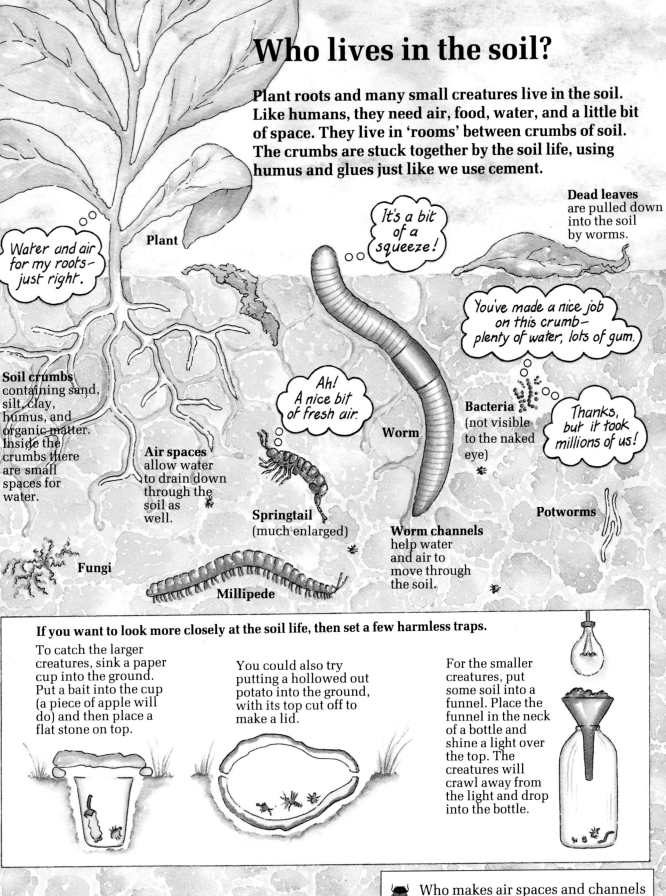

Plant

It's a bit of a squeeze!

Dead leaves are pulled down into the soil by worms.

Water and air for my roots— just right.

You've made a nice job on this crumb— plenty of water, lots of gum.

Soil crumbs containing sand, silt, clay, humus, and organic matter. Inside the crumbs there are small spaces for water.

Ah! A nice bit of fresh air.

Bacteria (not visible to the naked eye)

Thanks, but it took millions of us!

Worm

Air spaces allow water to drain down through the soil as well.

Springtail (much enlarged)

Worm channels help water and air to move through the soil.

Potworms

Fungi

Millipede

If you want to look more closely at the soil life, then set a few harmless traps.

To catch the larger creatures, sink a paper cup into the ground. Put a bait into the cup (a piece of apple will do) and then place a flat stone on top.

You could also try putting a hollowed out potato into the ground, with its top cut off to make a lid.

For the smaller creatures, put some soil into a funnel. Place the funnel in the neck of a bottle and shine a light over the top. The creatures will crawl away from the light and drop into the bottle.

 Who makes air spaces and channels through the soil?

The soil life circle

**Here are some of the creatures which can be found in the soil.
Use the circle to identify what you have found and
discover which creatures are the most common in your garden.**

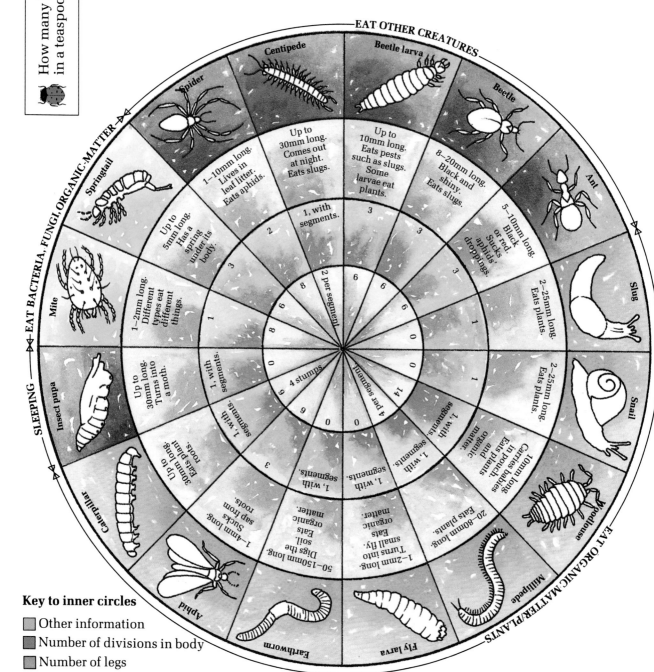

Key to inner circles

- Other information
- Number of divisions in body
- Number of legs

The soil nursery Several types of fly, beetle, and moth start their life in the soil as grubs called larvae. Before emerging above ground as adults, each larva forms a cocoon (or pupa) inside which its body changes dramatically. If you find a pupa, then put it on to some moist soil inside a dark box. Keep an eye on it and see what emerges!

Too small to see Soil bacteria and fungi are very small. A quarter of a million bacteria could fit on to the full stop at the end of this sentence. There are more bacteria in a teaspoon of soil than there are people on this planet.

Many of these creatures are useful; they are 'rotters' and eat the organic matter after the larger creatures have had a good chew first.

Earthworms

Worms are one of the most important types of soil creature.

Worm facts

A plot 10 × 10m in size contains about 2,500 worms with ½ km of tunnels.

Worms eat their own weight in organic matter and minerals each day.

Worm channels let water, roots, and air move through the soil.

Worm-casts are stuck together with gum and contain lots of plant food.

Worms come out on warm, damp evenings. They do not like light.

Worms move by squeezing their muscles and have bristles to stop them from slipping.

Worms are strong. Hold one in your loosely clenched fist and feel it push its way out between your fingers.

Worms often leave their back end in the burrow. If you touch them, then they shoot back underground.

If a worm is cut in half, only the half with the saddle (the fatter pink piece) will survive.

One worm is both male and female. When worms mate they swop sperm to fertilize the eggs, which they lay in the soil.

Some worms curl up and sleep in the summer when it is hot and dry.

Worms can live from several months to ten years.

Making a wormery

Put layers of damp soil, leaves, and sand into a jar. Add about twenty worms and put the jar in a dark place.

Look at the jar after a few days and see how the layers have been mixed up.

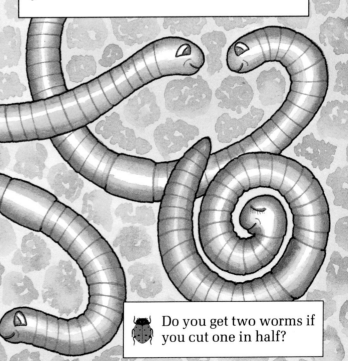

Do you get two worms if you cut one in half?

Feeding the soil

Organic matter helps plants in the soil to grow strong and healthy. It needs to rot a little before you add it to the soil.

Making compost

You can help your organic matter to rot by making compost, which is rather like baking a cake.

❶ The ingredients should include a good mixture of soft, sappy materials and tough, stemmy ones. Anything that was once alive can go on to the heap. However, be careful as fish and meat can attract rats! Mix your ingredients, chop them, and either make them into a heap and cover this with a piece of old carpet or, to speed things up, put them into a special tumbler like the one shown here. ❷ Many creatures, including bacteria, turn the mixture into compost. They eat the sappy material which gives them energy to chew on the stemmy bits. They need air and water to work, so turn the heap to get air into the mixture and water the heap to keep it moist. ❸ After a few weeks or months the mixture will have changed into a crumbly brown compost. This can then be dug into the soil or left on the surface for the worms to pull down.

Tough, stemmy materials

Straw   Paper   Stems (chopped)

Soft, sappy materials

Grass cuttings   Vegetable scraps   Feathers

After a few days, try putting your hand into the heap to see if it is warm.

All the creatures eating and working make it hot. This kills weed seeds and some plant diseases.

Making leaf mould

Throwing leaves away is a waste. Leaf mould is free and easy to make. It helps to build up the soil.

❶ Make a wire cage by stretching wire mesh around four posts which have been knocked into the ground. ❷ Fill the cage or a bin liner with soggy leaves and push them down. ❸ To speed things up, add some grass mowings. After one or two years the leaf mould will be ready.

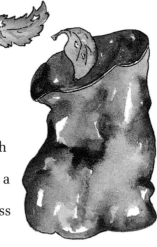

Making a wormbin

To make a wormbin, fill a large bin in the way shown here. When it is full, leave the bin until all the kitchen waste has been eaten and turned into brown, crumbly worm compost. This can be put on to the soil or used in potting compost.

Red brandling worms The worms used in a wormbin are called brandling worms. These red worms eat kitchen waste and turn it into worm compost, which is food for the soil and plants. You can get these worms from a fishing shop or from someone's compost bin.

Put a lid on the bin to keep flies out.

Water the surface if the mixture gets dry.

Worms like to be warm, so keep the bin away from cold winds and frost.

Cover the waste with newspaper to prevent any smell.

Add a little chopped waste every day (except meat or orange peel).

Put the worms in some leaf mould or strawy manure.

Drill holes near the bottom to let water escape (ask an adult for help with this).

Place a board, with some small holes in it, on to the gravel.

Put some gravel in the bottom.

Other organic matter

You can feed and help to build the soil with other sorts of organic matter.
❶ Strawy cow or horse manure can be put on to the soil after rotting. Manure from chickens and rabbits is very strong and should be put on to the compost heap to let the bacteria sort it out first. ❷ Mushroom compost is made from composted straw and manure. It is used for growing mushrooms. After the mushrooms have been picked, the compost can be put on to the garden. ❸ Peat is made from plants in wet boggy areas. Here, it provides a home for many beautiful and some rare plants and animals. This home is destroyed if the peat is dug up to use on the garden. There are now other products available that you can use instead of peat.

A heap of animal manure covered with plastic to stop nutrients being lost.

 Which manures are too strong to be put straight on to the garden?

How do plants work?

Plants are alive, just like humans. They give you oxygen to breathe and food to eat. Organic gardeners like to know how plants work so that they can help them to grow.

Plants take sunlight into their leaves. They use this to turn carbon dioxide (a gas) and water into sugar. Sugar is like a battery of energy. This process is called photosynthesis.

Leaves are flat and thin so that they catch as much sunlight as possible.

Sugar travels to all parts of the plant to give it energy to grow. It is also used to build up the plant's structure. Sugar that is not used is stored by the plant as starch. Potatoes are made of starch. Can you think of any other plant stores?

Flowers attract insects, which help the seeds to form and make new plants.

During the day, plants give off lots of water vapour from their leaves.

You breathe out carbon dioxide, which the leaves take in. So, talking to plants helps them to grow.

Leaves give out oxygen during the day, which lets you breathe. You could not live without plants.

Roots take up water from the soil to help make sugar and to make them rigid. If they do not get enough water, then they will go floppy and wilt. Sunflower roots can have a total length of 350m.

Roots need to take up plant foods from the soil. These are called nutrients.

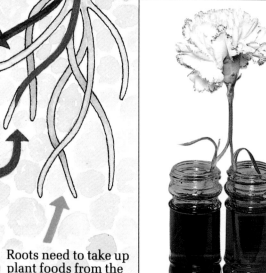

Watching plants take up water
Take a white carnation and split the stem into two. Put one half into blue ink and the other half into red ink. Watch the flower over a few days and see what happens.
　Plants usually take up water through their roots. The roots need to drink and breathe at the same time, so the soil needs to have air and water in it. The warmer it is, the more water vapour a plant gives off and the more water it needs to take in.

 Who feeds the plants?

Why do plants need the sun?

Plants need sunlight to grow, and they will even go looking for it. Put some moist soil into three pots and sow some seeds such as radishes in each, just below the soil surface. Keep the soil moist and watch what happens when the seedlings come up.

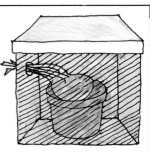

Put a sprouting potato into a shallow pot of moist soil. Cut a hole 3cm across in the side of a shoe box. Put the potato inside, put on the lid, and then place the box in a light place. Look in it after several weeks. Where is the shoot growing and what colour is it?

Put one pot outside (if it is spring or summer).

Put one pot on an inside window-sill.

Put one pot in a dark place.

Outside The seedlings are strong and healthy.

Inside The seedlings bend towards the sun. Turn the pot around and see what happens.

Dark place The seedlings are desperately looking for the light. Eventually they will run out of energy and die.

What do plants need to eat?

Many soil creatures eat organic matter and turn it into plant food. They are experts and give the plants the right amount of food at the right time. With chemical fertilizers it is easy to give the plants too much or the wrong balance of food. So, to feed your plants well all you have to do is look after the soil life and the soil.

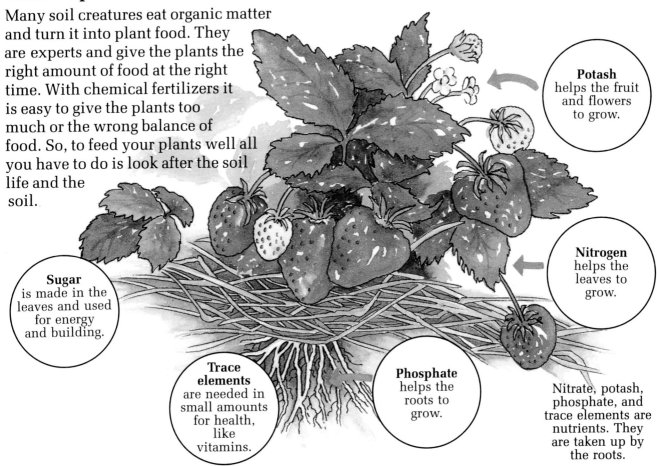

Potash helps the fruit and flowers to grow.

Nitrogen helps the leaves to grow.

Sugar is made in the leaves and used for energy and building.

Trace elements are needed in small amounts for health, like vitamins.

Phosphate helps the roots to grow.

Nitrate, potash, phosphate, and trace elements are nutrients. They are taken up by the roots.

Nitrogen, the leaf maker

Nitrogen helps plant leaves to grow. The air around you contains lots of nitrogen (78%) but plants cannot use it as a gas. They have to suck it up as nitrates through their roots. Nitrate fertilizer can be bought in bags, but organic gardeners do not use this as it can make plants too sappy. Their soil friends make nitrates from compost or the air. This is free and easy!

Clover is a green manure. This is a plant that is grown and dug back into the soil to feed it. This is not as crazy as it sounds, as some gases from the air are turned into organic matter by the clover. If you have some spare ground, then sow some clover. It will cover the soil, dig the ground with its roots, and make plant food. When you need the ground, dig in the clover, let it rot, and then plant your crops.

Legumes are plants like peas, beans, or clover. They make nitrogen fertilizer out of air. Pea and bean roots are covered in little lumps called nodules (see the picture below). These are factories where special bacteria live and work. They turn nitrogen from the air into plant food. The plant pays them with a home and sugar from its leaves.

 What is a green manure?

Plant tonics

Like humans, plants get tired or peaky. To pep them up you can use a tonic. Solid tonics (organic fertilizers) are put on to the soil, whilst liquids are watered on to the soil or the plant on a cloudy day.

 What nutrients do hoof and horn and bone meal give? (Page 13 may help you.)

SOLID TONICS

Organic fertilizers come from animals, plants, or natural rocks. You can buy them from most garden stores.

Hoof and horn helps leaves to grow.

Bone meal helps roots to grow.

Wood ash helps fruit and flowers to grow.

Seaweed is a general tonic.

Blood, fish and bone helps roots and leaves to grow.

Ground lime builds up the soil, makes clays less sticky, and helps plants feed in acid soil.

LIQUID TONICS

Liquid feeds come from plants such as comfrey and nettles. To make your own, you will need about 700g of either comfrey or nettle leaves.

Comfrey

Nettles

Put them into a bucket, fill it with water, and leave it to stand for four weeks. Strain the mixture before using it. It smells really awful but the soil and plants like it. To save space and the smell, try making the column shown below.

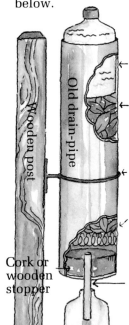

Old water-filled bottle (to weigh down the leaves)

Chopped leaves

Old drain-pipe

Wooden post

Bracket or rope (to hold the pipe up)

Wire mesh (to stop blockages)

Outer casing of a ball-point pen (ask an adult to drill a hole and put this into the stopper)

Cork or wooden stopper

Bottle (to catch the liquid)

Before using it, dilute the liquid using one part of liquid to twenty parts of water.

Getting started

Now it is time to get down to some real gardening. Ask at home, or at school, if you can have a small patch of garden. The pictures on this page will show you what you need to do.

1 Remove weeds by hand (see pages 34–5).

2 You can also cover the soil with black plastic or carpet to kill weeds, but this takes much longer (see pages 34–5).

3 After removing the weeds, dig the ground if it is not crumbly already.

4 Make beds ● Mark out some plots (beds) twice as wide as your arm. ● Dig them over. ● That's it! As all the plants can be reached from the paths, there is no need to walk on the soil and squash it. This means that once the beds have been made they do not need to be dug again.

5 Add compost to feed the soil. The worms will dig it in (see pages 10–11).

6 Cover the soil when it is warm and damp, and leave it like this until you need to use it. You can use old carpet or black plastic. The soil life likes a roof on its home.

7 Plant seeds or plants in warm, damp soil (see page 18).

8 If the plants wilt, then water the soil. Make sure that the water gets right down to the roots.
   If the plant looks sick, then try adding a tonic (see page 15).

9 Keep the soil covered. After harvesting plants, sow a plant which covers the soil (green manure) or put the carpet back on.

 What is the advantage of a bed?

16

Sowing seeds in containers

Start off some seeds in trays and keep them indoors so that the young plants will be ready to plant outside when the weather is warm enough.

How to sow seeds in containers

❶ Fill a seed tray with moist seed compost. Press it down gently. ❷ Sprinkle seeds on the surface, about 1cm apart. Cover the seeds with a fine layer of seed compost (very tiny seeds can be left on the surface). Cover the tray with newspaper and put it somewhere warm for the seeds to germinate. ❸ As soon as the seedlings come up, move them to a sunny window-sill. Water the compost so that it is damp but not too wet. ❹ When the seedlings have four leaves, dig them out gently using a teaspoon or a seed label. Try to keep some soil on the tiny delicate roots. Always pick the plants up carefully, holding them by the leaves and not the stem which is easily squashed. Plant them in another tray 4cm apart to give them more room. This is called pricking out. ❺ Once the seedlings have grown a little more they need to get used to the outside world. Put the tray outside for a few hours each day. This is called hardening off. ❻ Plant them outside in moist soil when the weather is warm, usually in late spring. Make a small hole, just big enough for the roots and a little compost, and move the plants gently. Leave enough room between them, so that they each have enough space to grow to full size.

Ben is planting seeds to start off early indoors. Suitable plants to start off in this way include tomatoes, lettuces, and African and French marigolds.

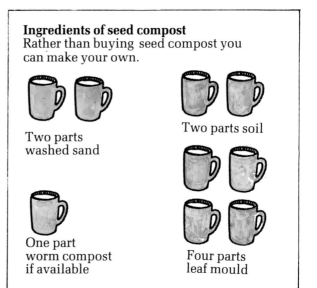

Ingredients of seed compost
Rather than buying seed compost you can make your own.

Two parts washed sand

Two parts soil

One part worm compost if available

Four parts leaf mould

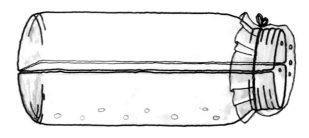

A large, clear plastic jar makes a seed tray and propagator all in one. Cut the jar in half lengthways. Poke holes in the bottom of one half and fill it with seed compost. After sowing, use the other half as a lid to keep the seedlings moist and warm.

Old yoghurt pots or margarine tubs make good pots and seed trays if a few holes are carefully poked in the base for drainage.

 What does pricking out mean?

Sowing seeds outside

Many seeds can go straight outside in the spring. You can collect some flower and vegetable seeds in the autumn. Put them in an envelope, label it, and keep the seeds dry and cool until sowing.

Seeds to collect in autumn

Flowers
Nasturtium
Love in a mist
Poached egg plant
Borage
Sunflower

Vegetables
Peas
Beans
Marrow
Leaf beet

How to sow seeds outside

❶ Make sure that the soil is weed-free, soft, and crumbly (see page 16). Gently rake the soil to get rid of any lumps. ❷ If you want to plant a row of seeds, then use a straight stick as a line and pull your finger through the soil to make a seed drill. Water the bottom of the drill. ❸ Sow the seeds thinly along the drill so that the seedlings will not be squashed together. Cover the seeds with fine, crumbly soil. Pat the soil down and label the row. ❹ Once the seedlings appear, thin them out so that the plants do not get overcrowded.

A rule of thumb
Sow seeds twice their own depth in the soil.

Sleeping seeds!
Some seeds go to sleep (lie dormant) and need a shock to wake them up. For example, primrose seeds need to be put in the refrigerator for a few weeks before they will grow!

Keeping seedlings warm
If it gets chilly, then keep your seedlings warm with a cloche. For one plant, cut an old plastic bottle in half to make a mini greenhouse.

For a row of plants, use some wire coat hangers. Ask an adult to cut them at the bottom, then bend them out and push them into the ground. Cover them with a sheet of clear plastic, and hold this down using some stones at the edges. Cloches keep out some pests as well as bad weather.

Why do you cover plants with a cloche?

Making plants from cuttings

Some plants can be grown from cuttings. A cutting is a piece of plant, usually a shoot, that has been cut off from the main plant. It must be helped to grow new roots so that it can survive on its own.

 How and why do you harden off a cutting? (Page 17 may help you.)

Softwood cuttings

These are soft and need gentle treatment. You can take softwood cuttings from plants such as Michaelmas daisies, thyme, and rosemary.

1 In the spring, take a soft stem about 10cm long and cut it off the parent plant just below a leaf.

2 Remove the lower leaves from the cutting.

3 Plant the cutting in cutting compost, made from 50% leaf mould and 50% grit. Treat the plant with care, as it has no roots yet!

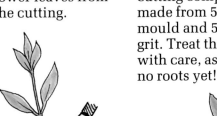

4 Put a plastic bag over it so that it does not lose too much water, and put it in a spot out of direct sunlight. Give the pot some gentle heat from underneath (you could place the plant over a warm radiator).

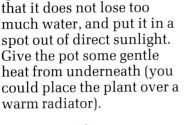

5 When the cutting starts to grow leaves, it means that it has rooted and needs to be repotted into potting compost. Make this by adding 100g of general organic fertilizer to a bucket of seed compost. Harden off the cutting before planting it outside.

Hardwood cuttings

These are hard and can be treated roughly!
You can take hardwood cuttings from plants such as willow, hawthorn, and blackcurrants.

1 When the plant is dormant, in the winter, cut a hard stem about 20cm long just below a bud.

2 Make a slit in the ground and put some sand in the bottom.
3 Push the cutting into the slit and cover it with soil to half its length.
4 Leave it outside for a year.
5 When the cutting grows leaves, it is ready to move to wherever you want it.

Other ways of making plants

There are lots of other ways of getting new plants.

◀ **Strawberries** produce new plants on long shoots called runners.

▲ **Honeysuckle** can be bent down and pegged to the ground. This is called layering. New roots will grow where the stem touches the soil. The layered piece can then be cut off and replanted.

▼ **Marguerites** can be dug up and the clump split in half and replanted.

▲ **Garlic** can be split into cloves and planted. Each one will grow into a clump.

 What is a runner?

What to grow and when

The plants that you grow in your garden originally came from all over the world. Wild plants discovered by gardeners and plant collectors have been bred and improved to give the wide range of vegetables, fruits, and flowers found today. The gardeners' calendar below will help you to plan the year ahead in your garden.

Did you know?
Both potatoes and runner beans originally came from South America! Try to discover the origin of your favourite vegetable (your local library is a good place to start).

SEASON	WHAT TO SOW	WHAT TO PLANT	OTHER THINGS TO DO
Spring	**Inside** Pumpkins, marrows, French beans, lettuces, tomatoes. **Outside** Peas, beans, radishes, lettuces, clover as a green manure. Sunflowers, corn marigolds, wallflowers, love in a mist, nasturtiums, poached egg plants.	Early potatoes, garlic, lettuce raised inside.	Dig and make beds. Add compost. Layer honeysuckle. Take softwood cuttings. Watch for pests.
Summer	Pumpkins, marrows, French beans, radishes, lettuces, parsley. Honesty, wallflowers.	Pumpkins, marrows, French beans, tomatoes. Flowers raised inside.	Make nettle/comfrey liquid. Watch for pests. Water if dry. Weed.
Autumn	Radishes, winter lettuces (under a cloche), winter rye (a green manure), mustard and cress inside.	Trees, shrubs. Strawberry runners. Bulbs, wallflowers, ice plants.	Harvest vegetables before the frosts. Dig and make beds. Add compost. Take hardwood cuttings. Prune blackcurrants. Divide plants. Make leaf mould.
Winter	Mustard and cress inside.	Trees, shrubs. Garlic.	Dig and make beds. Make pot-pourri for Christmas. Plan the garden. Clean tools. Warm beds with cloches. Sprout potatoes in egg boxes.

What is a cutting?
(Page 19 may help you.)

Crop rotation

It is a good idea to grow different families of vegetables in separate plots and move them around (rotate them) each year. This helps to keep soil pests and diseases under control, and it makes the best use of your valuable compost.

You can sow a green manure, such as clover, in a plot that is not being used.

PLOT 1
Potato
family

PLOT 2
Root
family

YEAR 1

PLOT 4
Legume
family

PLOT 3
Brassica
family

PLOT 1
Legume
family

PLOT 2
Potato
family

YEAR 2

PLOT 4
Brassica
family

PLOT 3
Root
family

PLOT 1
Brassica
family

PLOT 2
Legume
family

YEAR 3

PLOT 4
Root
family

PLOT 3
Potato
family

PLOT 1
Root
family

PLOT 2
Brassica
family

YEAR 4

PLOT 4
Potato
family

PLOT 3
Legume
family

Can you identify the four vegetables shown in the rotation?

Easy growing projects

Growing your own vegetables is not difficult.

Potatoes

Potatoes are swollen stems that store the potato plant's food underground. Growing them is usually hard work, because they need earth piled over their new shoots to stop the new potatoes turning green in the light. Green potatoes are poisonous and should not be eaten. However, there is an easy way to grow potatoes.

If you are not able to find four old tyres, then try using only one. Lizzie found thirty-seven potatoes in this tyre, which had all grown from a single plant!

Growing potatoes in tyres

❶ Put a tyre on to the soil and fill it with compost. ❷ Sprout a potato by putting it on a warm window-sill in the spring. An early variety is best. When the sprouts are 1–3cm long, put the potato into the compost in the tyre. ❸ Water the sprouts every few days. When they are about 10cm long, put another tyre on top and fill it with soil. Keep watering, and as the potato continues to grow add more tyres and soil. ❹ When you have a pile of four tyres, leave the potato to flower but keep watering it if the soil is dry. ❺ When the flowers die, stop watering. Early potatoes are ready soon after the flowers have died, whilst maincrop potatoes are ready when the leaves begin to die. Take off the tyres and count how many potatoes you have grown.

Beans, mustard and cress

Even if you have no garden at all, you can grow mustard and cress or bean sprouts.

❶ Put some moist blotting paper on to a plate or into a large clear jar placed on its side. ❷ Add some mustard and cress seeds, mung beans, or alfalfa seed. ❸ Put the plate or jar on a sunny window-sill, keep the paper moist, and watch the seeds grow. ❹ Eat the mustard and cress seedlings and the bean sprouts when they are young. They taste delicious in a salad.

Is a potato a root or a stem?

23

Grow your own 'baked beans'

The best beans to use are 'Blue Lake' climbing French beans or 'Czar' runner beans. You can buy these from most garden centres. After the first year, you can save some beans to sow the following year. For the sauce, use an outdoor bush type of tomato, such as 'Red Alert'.

The sauce

❶ In the spring, fill some pots with seed compost (see page 17) and sow about five tomato seeds in each one. ❷ Keep the pots on a sunny window-sill and thin the seedlings to one per pot. Water them once a week with a liquid feed. ❸ Harden off the plants in early summer and plant them out into soil containing compost, or into containers filled with potting compost (see page 19). Support each plant with a cane pushed into the ground. ❹ Put a straw or newspaper covering around the plants to keep down weeds and keep the tomatoes off the ground. This is called a mulch. Water them when the soil is dry and tap the flowers gently to help them grow tomatoes. Also, give them a liquid feed each week. ❺ The tomatoes should be ready to pick at the end of the summer. Cut them up, cook them, and then mash them to make your tomato sauce!

The beans

❶ Grow the beans using the same methods as for the tomatoes. You will only need to sow two beans per pot because the seeds are bigger. ❷ When planting out, you will need some sticks 150cm long to support the plants because they grow quite tall. The sticks can be made into a wigwam shape and tied at the top with string. ❸ The beans will be ready to pick fresh in the summer (when they will only need boiling lightly) or dried in the autumn. If it is a wet year, then pick the bean pods before they are completely dry and hang them in a warm, dry shed. Take the beans out of the pods, soak them in water overnight, and then boil them until tender before adding your tomato sauce.

 Beans belong to the same family as peas. What is it called? (Pages 14 and 22 may help you.)

How do you tell which of a pumpkin's flowers are female ones?

Pumpkin seeds can be roasted and eaten, or saved for sowing the following year.
Pumpkin flesh makes lovely soup and pies.
Pumpkin shells, when hollowed out, make good lanterns for a bonfire party.

Pumpkins for Hallowe'en

Pumpkins take several months to grow but are well worth it. They are ready in the autumn, around Hallowe'en time and Bonfire Night.

❶ Sow the seeds in spring and grow them like the tomatoes and beans described on the opposite page. Pumpkins grow much larger if they are grown in a soil rich in garden compost. ❷ When the plants have five leaves, pinch out the tips. This will make them bushy. They will not need sticks or canes because the plants creep along the ground. ❸ If you want a big pumpkin, then look out for a small fruit swelling behind a flower (this is a female one) and put it on to a board to stop soil creatures from nibbling it. ❹ Cut off nearly all the other female flowers and water the plant well using a liquid feed once a week. ❺ You could have a competition with a friend to see who can grow the biggest pumpkin.

A fruitful harvest

Organic fruits and vegetables from your own garden are delicious and taste quite different from those that you can buy in the shops.

Fruits can be eaten fresh or made into pies and drinks. You can pick fresh fruit for most of the year.

Late spring Rhubarb and gooseberries (cookers).

Early summer Strawberries.

Midsummer Raspberries, gooseberries (eaters), and red, black, and white currants.

Late summer Blackberries, plums, and cherries.

Autumn Apples and pears.

Winter Stored apples and pears.

Strawberry time

Freshly picked strawberries are the sweetest! Strawberry runners can be planted in the summer, and newly planted ones will produce fruit for three to four summers.

❶ Plant the runners on soil that is not compacted (squashed down) and give them plenty of well-rotted manure. A sprinkling of bone meal and seaweed meal on the soil will also help them to grow strong and healthy. ❷ When the fruits are nearly ripe, put some straw under them to keep them clean. If you have some comfrey leaves, then push these under the straw to feed the plants. ❸ Cut off new runners if you do not want new plants (this makes the parent plant grow larger strawberries). ❹ Strawberries are very popular with the garden wildlife too. The straw will keep the slugs off and an old net curtain laid over the ripening fruit will keep blackbirds away. ❺ After the fruit has finished, cut off the old leaves, carefully leaving the new shoots (the crown) in the middle. This helps to prevent the strawberry plants from getting diseases.

Blackcurrants

You can grow a blackcurrant from a hardwood cutting, as shown on page 19.

❶ Plant your cutting in the autumn. Choose a sunny position in well-dug soil which contains plenty of compost and manure. Some bone meal in the bottom of the hole will help new roots to grow. Also, put some feathers out of an old pillow, or some hoof and horn fertilizer, into the hole to give the bush the nitrogen that it needs.

❷ Blackcurrants grow on wood that is a year old. To get lots of one year old shoots, ask an adult to help you cut out one third of the old wood close to the ground each autumn. New shoots will grow from the base. This is called pruning. ❸ Other types of fruit bushes and trees are pruned in different ways. Can you discover how? (An adult gardening book may help you.)

 In the picture above, Anish and Jonathan are pruning a blackcurrant bush. What are the two things that they are doing wrong?

Let's have a drink

You can make your own fruit squash from blackcurrants. Ask an adult to help you because fruits get very hot when they are cooked.

❶ Pick 500g of blackcurrants and gently simmer them with about a cupful of water. Use a potato masher to squash the currants, and then boil the mixture for a couple of minutes. ❷ Pour the mixture into a jelly bag, hang it up and let it drip into a clean bowl. Add sugar to taste whilst the mixture is warm enough for it to dissolve. ❸ Bottle and dilute it to taste like fruit squash. Because the squash does not contain any chemicals to stop it going off, keep it in the refrigerator. You can also make it into ice-cubes.

Growing herbs

Herbs are plants that are useful for their taste, their smell, or their medicinal properties. They are used in very small amounts. You can grow your own herbs in a container such as an old washing-up bowl, a large flower-pot, or half of an old tyre. Most herbs will keep coming up year after year.

Caring for herbs
● Water them if the soil dries out. ● Clip them to encourage new growth. ● Feed them with a liquid feed during the summer. ● Pull out any weeds that appear.

Parsley This is grown from seed. The seeds take a long time to get started, so put them in a warm place once sown.

Rosemary Grow this from a softwood cutting and keep it well clipped so that it does not get straggly.

Sage This is grown from a softwood cutting. Keep it well clipped so that it does not get straggly.

Chive This is grown from seed or by division. It has pretty purple flowers. The leaves have a mild onion flavour.

Thyme Grow this from seed, from a softwood cutting, or by division. Thyme attracts many insects.

Chervil This is grown from seed. The leaves have an aniseed taste.

Borage This is grown from seed. It has pretty blue flowers, and the fresh leaves and flowers have a cucumber flavour.

Marjoram This is grown from seed or by division. Pot marjoram is the easiest to grow.

Mint Grow this in organic potting compost from pieces of root or by the division of a large plant. Keep it in a separate pot as it grows and spreads very quickly!

Bay This is grown from a softwood cutting. It can be a little difficult to get it started.

Preparing the container
❶ Make some holes in the bottom of the container for drainage. ❷ Put a layer of broken pots or gravel in the bottom. ❸ Fill the container with a good mixture of soil and compost. Add some grit to help drainage.

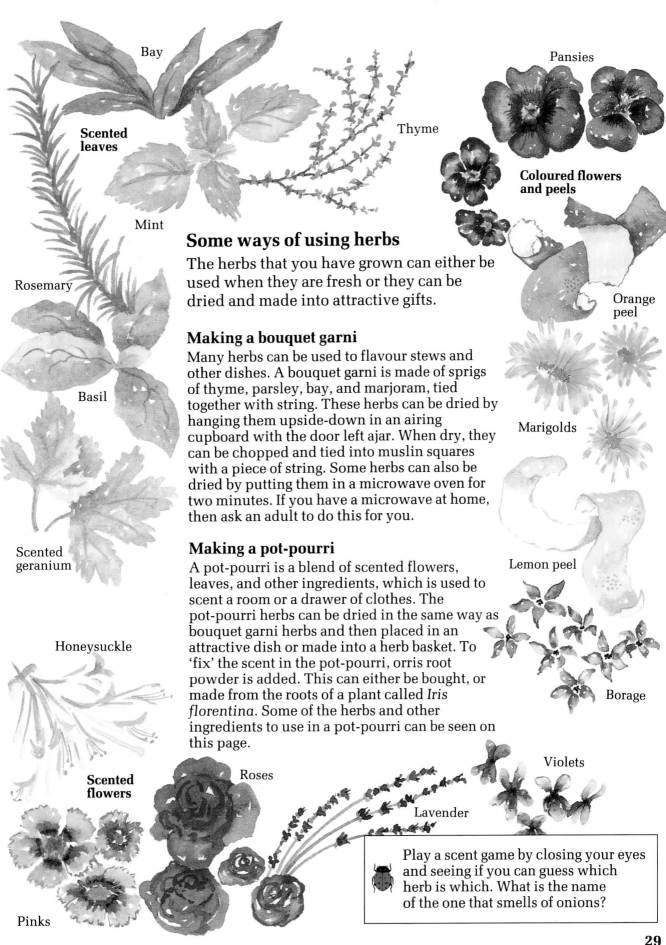

Bay

Scented leaves

Thyme

Mint

Rosemary

Basil

Scented geranium

Honeysuckle

Scented flowers

Roses

Pinks

Pansies

Coloured flowers and peels

Orange peel

Marigolds

Lemon peel

Borage

Violets

Lavender

Some ways of using herbs

The herbs that you have grown can either be used when they are fresh or they can be dried and made into attractive gifts.

Making a bouquet garni

Many herbs can be used to flavour stews and other dishes. A bouquet garni is made of sprigs of thyme, parsley, bay, and marjoram, tied together with string. These herbs can be dried by hanging them upside-down in an airing cupboard with the door left ajar. When dry, they can be chopped and tied into muslin squares with a piece of string. Some herbs can also be dried by putting them in a microwave oven for two minutes. If you have a microwave at home, then ask an adult to do this for you.

Making a pot-pourri

A pot-pourri is a blend of scented flowers, leaves, and other ingredients, which is used to scent a room or a drawer of clothes. The pot-pourri herbs can be dried in the same way as bouquet garni herbs and then placed in an attractive dish or made into a herb basket. To 'fix' the scent in the pot-pourri, orris root powder is added. This can either be bought, or made from the roots of a plant called *Iris florentina*. Some of the herbs and other ingredients to use in a pot-pourri can be seen on this page.

Play a scent game by closing your eyes and seeing if you can guess which herb is which. What is the name of the one that smells of onions?

Garden flowers and shrubs

Flowers are an important part of a natural garden. Some are useful as they help to control pests, some are edible, and others just look nice.

Hardy annuals

Grow these from seed outside in the spring. Hardy annuals flower and die in one year. However, their seeds will survive outside all through the winter and grow into new plants the following spring.

▼ **French marigold** This keeps some pests off your plants. The seeds need to be started off indoors.

▲ **Borage** This attracts bees. The flowers can be put into drinks to make a summer cocktail.

◀ **Poached egg plant** This attracts hover-flies, whose babies (larvae) eat pests.

Biennials

Grow these from seed outside in the summer. Biennials take two years to flower and then die.

▶ **Honesty** This is an early flowering plant which attracts the orange-tip butterfly. The seed pods are very attractive and look like thin silver pennies.

▲ **Wallflower** This is a perfumed flower which attracts the butterflies that appear in spring.

Herbaceous perennials

These live for more than three years. They die back each winter and reappear in the spring.

▼ **Michaelmas daisy** This provides food for small copper and tortoise-shell butterflies in the autumn.

▲ **Ice plant** This provides food for tortoise-shell butterflies before they go to sleep (hibernate) in late autumn.

◀ **Daffodil** Ornamental daffodils bring brightness into a spring garden. Plant the bulbs in the autumn, in twice their own depth of soil.

Woody perennials

These live for more than three years and have woody stems.

▼ **Hydrangea** This clever shrub has pink flowers in alkaline soils and blue flowers in acid soils.

◀ **Honeysuckle** The beautifully perfumed flowers of this plant attract moths at night. If you bite the base of the flower, then you can taste the sweet nectar which is their food.

▼ **Buddleia** The flowers of this shrub are often covered with butterflies.

▶ **Oak** This tree provides a home for hundreds of different birds and insects. The branch shown has marble galls, which are the home of tiny wasps.

What is the difference between an annual plant and a biennial plant?

Flower power

Flowers are a very important part of the plant because they produce the seeds. Their different shapes, colours, and smells are especially designed to attract insects, which bring pollen from other flowers to help the seeds develop.

Sunflowers

These are so named because they turn their faces to look at the sun. They can grow up to 4m tall and will flower in late summer.

1 In the spring, sow some seeds 1cm deep in seed compost. Keep them on a sunny window-sill and water them every few days. **2** When the plants are about 10cm tall, plant them in a sunny spot in the garden. **3** Stake the plants to support them and measure them each week. You could have a competition with friends to see who can grow the tallest sunflower. **4** After flowering, the sunflower produces lots of seeds. These can be shelled and eaten, or saved for sowing the following year.

Nasturtiums

These come from Peru. They are annuals, growing from seed each year.

● The seeds can be planted in well-prepared ground in the spring. ● The leaves can be eaten in salads and taste peppery. ● The beautiful yellow and red trumpet-shaped flowers are edible and also attract useful insects which eat pests.

Why do plants have flowers?

Wild flowers

The garden can be a home not only for your garden flowers, fruits, and vegetables, but also for a variety of wild flowers.

Look after them!

Many wild flowers are becoming rare, being destroyed by such things as chemical farming and building work. If you have room in your garden, then you could grow some wild flowers, either in a border or with grasses in a meadow. Many will attract useful wildlife to help control pests.

Never pick or pull up flowers from the wild. You can easily buy or collect a few seeds and it is much more interesting to grow them yourself.

◀ **Wild orchids** are becoming very rare. They take many years to flower and are difficult to grow from seed.

 Why should you not pick wild flowers?

DIFFERENT PLANTS FOR DIFFERENT PLACES

Damp soil in sun

Celandine
Cuckoo flower
Meadowsweet
Hemp agrimony
◀ **Purple loosestrife**
Ragged robin

Dry soil in sun

Bird's-foot trefoil
Cowslip
◀ **Wild pansy**
Field scabious
Harebell
Ox-eye daisy
◀ **Cornflower**

Damp soil in shade

Bluebell
Foxglove
◀ **Primrose**
Ramsons (smell like garlic)

Dry soil in shade

Violet
Red campion
◀ **Wood anemone**
Wood sorrel

Weeds

A weed is a plant in the wrong place. The main reason for pulling weeds out is because they want the same things as your crop plants, e.g. water, food, and light.

Keeping weeds under control

There are several things that you can do to control weeds.

❶ First of all, hoe and pull up all the weeds in your garden. Make sure that you hoe when it is dry, or the clever weeds will root again. When pulling them up, try to get all of the root up.

● After hoeing, the soil will still be full of weed seeds. Some have been there for ages and just need a little light to get them started. Others you will have brought in yourself. The next time that you go for a walk in the country, scrape the mud off your boots into a seed tray and see what comes up. One gardener managed to grow forty-three species of weed from the mud on his boot, and a real weed enthusiast, Sir Edward Salisbury, raised three hundred plants from the debris that he pulled out of his trouser turn-ups!

❷ If you find all the hoeing and pulling hard work, then try this! Weeds need light to grow, so do not give them any. Put your plants in the ground quite close together so that when they are fully grown there will be no room for the weeds.

❸ Another way to kill weeds is to cover the ground with a mulch. Things that you can use include grass mowings, hay, straw, wood bark, and wood chips. Some crops, like pumpkins, can be planted through holes made in the mulch, so that you can grow the plants that you want and keep the weeds off at the same time, without any hard work.

WEED PROBLEMS	WEED USES
✕ Weeds compete with your plants for light, water, and food.	√ Weeds attract useful wildlife to the garden.
✕ Some weeds can attack plants (couch grass can grow right through potatoes).	√ Weeds can show you what kind of soil you have, e.g. nettles show that the soil is good and silver-weed shows that it can be wet and difficult to dig.
✕ Weeds can hurt, e.g. nettles!	√ Weed leaves make good compost.
✕ Weeds can look ugly in amongst the flowers.	√ Some weeds are edible, e.g. sorrel.
✕ Weeds can spread pests.	√ Many weeds are beautiful to look at.

How weeds spread

Weeds are really very clever plants which multiply rapidly, spread quickly, and fight back when you try to chop them up.

Why does covering the soil kill weeds?

▼ **Ragwort** seeds can be carried over 100km by the wind.

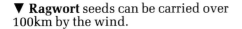

▲ **Plantains** change shape. They grow tall in long grass and flat on mown lawns to avoid the mower blades.

◄ **Bindweed** roots can creep under the soil unseen and spread 25 sq m in a year.

▲ **Chickweed** plants can produce 15,000 million plants a year from seed!

◄ **Dandelion** roots can grow into new plants even when they have been chopped up.

Poisonous plants

Some of the plants that you find in the garden or in the wild are poisonous.
Never eat them, and if you touch them then always wash your hands afterwards. Some of the ones to avoid are shown here, but there are many others and you should never eat anything until you are sure of what it is.

❶ Yew *Taxus baccata* (the berries are poisonous)
❷ Sun spurge *Euphorbia helioscopia* (the sap can cause blisters)
❸ Autumn crocus *Colchicum*
❹ Potato *Solanum tuberosum* (when green)
❺ Laburnum *Laburnum anagyroides*
❻ Elder *Sambucus nigra* (the raw berries are poisonous)
❼ Foxglove *Digitalis purpurea*
❽ Fly agaric *Amanita muscaria*
❾ Arum *Arum maculatum* (cuckoo pint, lords and ladies)

When are potatoes poisonous?

Animal life in the garden

Your garden is a home for many wild creatures. Some of them will help to keep the pests off your plants. Like people, they need food, water, shelter, and somewhere quiet and safe to raise their young.

Attracting wildlife

There are many things that you can do to attract and look after the animals in your garden.

● **Growing organically** Chemical sprays not only harm the pests, but also the creatures that feed on them. ● **Growing food plants** Grow these for the wildlife as well as for yourself. ● **Making a pond** Make this for the creatures that live in the water, and as a drinking place for others. ● **Providing shelter** Make log piles for the small creatures and grow shrubs for the larger ones such as birds and voles. ● **Not being too tidy** Leave some weeds in a corner for the wildlife, or let some of the grass grow to form a small meadow for butterflies. ● **Providing a corridor** Make sure that there is a 'corridor', or passageway, of wild plants into the wildlife garden to let creatures in and out.

Creatures depend upon one another for food. By attracting small creatures, such as insects and snails, you will provide a food source for other visitors to the garden. A very simple food web is shown here. Can you find any other food webs in your garden?

What is an insectivorous bird?

Food plants

Plants provide food in a number of ways.

❶ Caterpillars and other insects eat certain leaves. Butterflies find these leaves by smell, and lay their eggs on leaves facing the sun. Plants for egg-laying butterflies and moths include nettles, mullien, alder, ash, vetch, sorrel, honesty, and rosebay willowherb.

❷ Insectivorous birds, such as blue tits, thrushes, robins, and blackbirds, eat the insects attracted by the plants.

❸ Butterflies, hover-flies, and other insects sip nectar from flowers, and bees collect pollen from them. Butterflies seem to like the pink and purple flowers (see above), whilst hover-flies go for the yellows and golds.

❹ Some plants, such as pyracantha, cotoneaster, guelder rose (see above), hawthorn, dog rose, thistle, and hazel, provide seeds, nuts, and berries for certain birds and small mammals. The best way to see which creatures eat which plants is to sit quietly in the garden and watch.

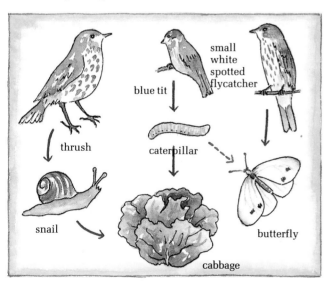

small white spotted flycatcher

blue tit

thrush

caterpillar

snail

butterfly

cabbage

Garden habitats

Although most wild creatures do not live in homes like people, they do need places to shelter from bad weather and also to raise their young. The ideas given here will help you to create more habitats in your garden or at school.

Shelter for the small ones

Log piles make excellent shelters for the smaller wildlife in the garden, such as ground beetles. They also provide a hibernation place for toads. Both these creatures eat garden pests, such as slugs and ants, so a log pile will help to protect your garden plants! As your log pile begins to rot you will also see mosses and fungi growing all over it.

Food and shelter

Hedges, or even a few native shrubs planted together, provide shelter and food for birds and other animals. Shrubs such as sloe, buckthorn, crab apple (pictured above), dog rose, field maple, hawthorn, hazel, and wayfaring tree are all suitable.

Plant shrubs in the autumn or winter when they are dormant. ❶ Dig a hole big enough for the roots to be spread out and mix a small amount of compost and bone meal in the hole. ❷ Plant the shrub up to the soil mark on the stem, then firm the ground and water it. ❸ Place an old piece of carpet or black plastic around the shrub to keep down weeds and keep in water.

Making a nesting site

Small birds, such as tits, wrens, and sparrows, may nest in your garden if you provide them with a tit box. Any wooden box that is about 10cm square will do. The box needs to be completely enclosed, with a hole 30mm in diameter in the side. An attractive box can be made from a log which is split in half and then hollowed out and strapped back together. (Adult help will be needed!) The box needs to be attached to a tree or a wall at least 2m above the ground to keep out cats. Try to watch the birds building their nest or feeding their young.

Looking after hedgehogs

To attract hedgehogs, you can make a nest like the one shown here. Hedgehogs need a place like this to hibernate through the cold winter months and to use for breeding. They are very useful because they eat slugs.

 What does hibernate mean? (Page 31 may help you.)

Encouraging pond-life

A pond is a very valuable habitat in the natural garden. It provides a useful water supply for garden wildlife, a home for frogs and newts, and a hunting ground for insectivorous creatures.

Take care! Ponds can be dangerous. Never play around them unless you have an adult with you.

Frogs Garden ponds have saved the frog from becoming extinct. Frogs spend most of their adult life on land (eating slugs in the garden). In the spring, they mate and lay frog-spawn in ponds. The frog-spawn develops into tadpoles, which eat plants at first and then 'meat' as they develop legs and start to breathe air. They leave the pond as small adults (froglets) and it is three years before they come back to breed.

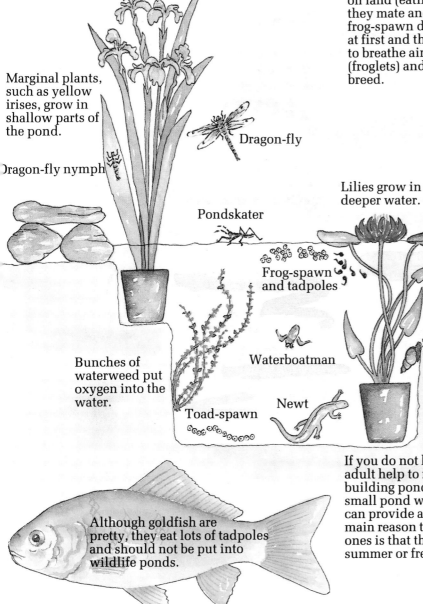

Marginal plants, such as yellow irises, grow in shallow parts of the pond.

Dragon-fly nymph

Dragon-fly

Pondskater

Lilies grow in deeper water.

Frogs hibernate under rocks.

Frog-spawn and tadpoles

Animals use the gentle slope to get in and out of the pond.

Bunches of waterweed put oxygen into the water.

Waterboatman

Toad-spawn

Newt

Ramshorn snails and great pond snails eat the algae and stop the pond from becoming murky.

If you do not have a pond, then you will need some adult help to make one. You could look for a book on building ponds in your local library. Even a very small pond will do, e.g. an old sink or plastic bowl can provide a home for froglets and water snails. The main reason that large ponds are better than small ones is that they are less likely to dry out in the summer or freeze over in the winter.

Although goldfish are pretty, they eat lots of tadpoles and should not be put into wildlife ponds.

 What is a marginal plant?

Friends and foes

These pictures will help you to distinguish the creatures in the garden that are friends from the ones that are foes. There are, of course, hundreds of creepy-crawlies in the garden and only a few can be shown here.

◀ **Hover-flies** (enlarged) eat nectar and lay their eggs near aphids. Their larvae, which look like bird droppings, eat aphids.

▼ **Lacewings** chew up aphids, whilst their larvae suck them dry. The larvae pile the dead carcasses on their backs – ugh!

▲ **Ladybirds** (much enlarged) and their larvae (enlarged) eat aphids. There are many types: the seven spot, the two spot, and the twenty-two spot (which is yellow and black) are the most common.

◀ **Caterpillars**, like the cabbage white ones shown here, can damage crops.

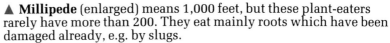

▲ **Millipede** (enlarged) means 1,000 feet, but these plant-eaters rarely have more than 200. They eat mainly roots which have been damaged already, e.g. by slugs.

▲ **Earwigs** (enlarged) eat whatever they can get their jaws on, plant or animal. So, as well as nibbling the odd plant, they also do away with pests such as codling moth eggs (the maggots in apples).

▶ **Wasps** (much enlarged) can be a nuisance in late summer, when they are looking for sticky, sweet things to eat. However, earlier in the year they are useful friends, gathering insects for the young wasp grubs to eat. The wasps in one nest can eat over 250,000 insect pests a year.

Key
△ Friend
▲ Foe
△ Friend or foe?

 Do hover-flies eat aphids?

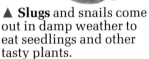
Aphids (much enlarged) come in many shapes and sizes, and in great numbers. It has been estimated that there can be up to 500,000 aphids in a square metre! They have mouths like straws and plug into the sugary sap of plants. The sugar that they cannot eat drips straight out of their back ends (honeydew). This makes the plants go sticky and then mouldy.

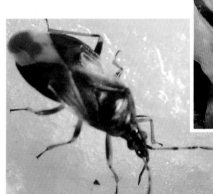

▲ **Slugs** and snails come out in damp weather to eat seedlings and other tasty plants.

▶ **Anthocorids** (much enlarged) are tiny flower bugs. They are good at eating aphids and can also nip you if they land on your hand!

▼ **Ground beetles** (enlarged) are one of the most useful types of creature in the garden. They scuttle on the soil and leaf litter, and will even climb plants in search of slugs and caterpillars.

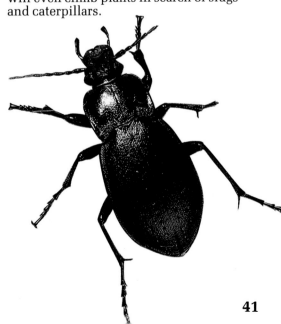

▲ **Centipedes** (enlarged) eat anything that they can get their fangs on, including slugs, but they do not like millipedes much.

Controlling pests

Organic gardeners control their pests by encouraging predators and parasites, and by using tricks and traps. No chemicals are used, because these can kill not only the pests but also the creatures that eat the pests.

The gory story

Pests breed quickly and one aphid can produce one million babies in a month. If it were not for their enemies, then your garden would be overrun in no time.

The pictures on pages 40 and 41 show lots of examples of friendly predators, which are creatures that gobble up pests! Here are some examples of parasites, which are creatures that actually make their homes on or inside a pest and slowly eat it to live.

▼ **Parasitic wasps in aphids** The adult wasps lay their eggs inside the aphids. The aphids then turn straw-coloured and fat as the parasites grow inside and eat them. When their meal is over the wasps saw a hole and pop out.

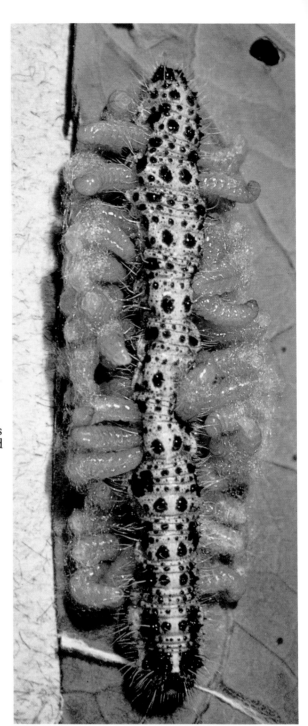

▲ **Parasitic wasps in a caterpillar** These little grubs have just come out of this caterpillar pest. The mother wasp lays her eggs inside the caterpillar and when the grubs hatch they eat their way out, keeping the caterpillar alive as long as possible.

 What is the difference between a predator and a parasite?

Traps and tricks

Controlling pests in the natural garden is exciting. It is just like a battle plan, where you can use brains against brawn.

1 Make sure that your soil is healthy and full of life to feed the plants. Healthy plants do not get so many pests. **2** Choose seeds that are resistant to certain problems. This is shown on the packet. **3** Rotate your crops (see page 22). **4** Grow plants that hide the crop from the pest by smell or sight. This is called companion planting. **5** Sow your crops when the pests are not around, e.g. peas sown in late winter or late spring avoid pea moth (where the caterpillar eats the peas inside the pod). **6** Attract predators by growing attractant plants, such as Californian poppies and Michaelmas daisies, and having many different habitats in your garden (see pages 37–9). **7** Make some traps and protect crops with barriers and scarers. Frighten off the enemy!

▼ **Carpet collars** Cabbage root fly grubs eat cabbage roots! However, if you put a collar of carpet around the roots then the fly cannot lay its eggs there. This is simple and very effective.

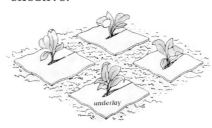

underlay

▲ **Nets and bottles** Cover plants with nets or plastic bottles with the bottoms cut off to keep off flying pests.

▲ **Prickles** Keep cats off seed-beds by putting rose prunings or something prickly where their paws would like to tread.

▲ **Scarers** Keep crop-eating birds off with scarers. Try making a scarecrow or a cardboard cut-out of a bird of prey stuck on to a stick. Old cassette tape strung up tightly between poles also frightens birds by the humming noise it makes.

▲ **Slug pub** Slugs like beer! Put some into a dish sunk into the ground and the slugs will drown.

▲ **Pheromones** Another trap which is available to control pests is a box that contains the perfume of a specific female moth. When the male moth flies into the box, in search of his sweetheart, all he comes to is a sticky end as the box is full of perfume and glue. This keeps the moths from mating, the eggs from being laid, and the caterpillars from eating your apples and pears.

The bean game

To play this game you will need a dice and some large seeds to use as counters.

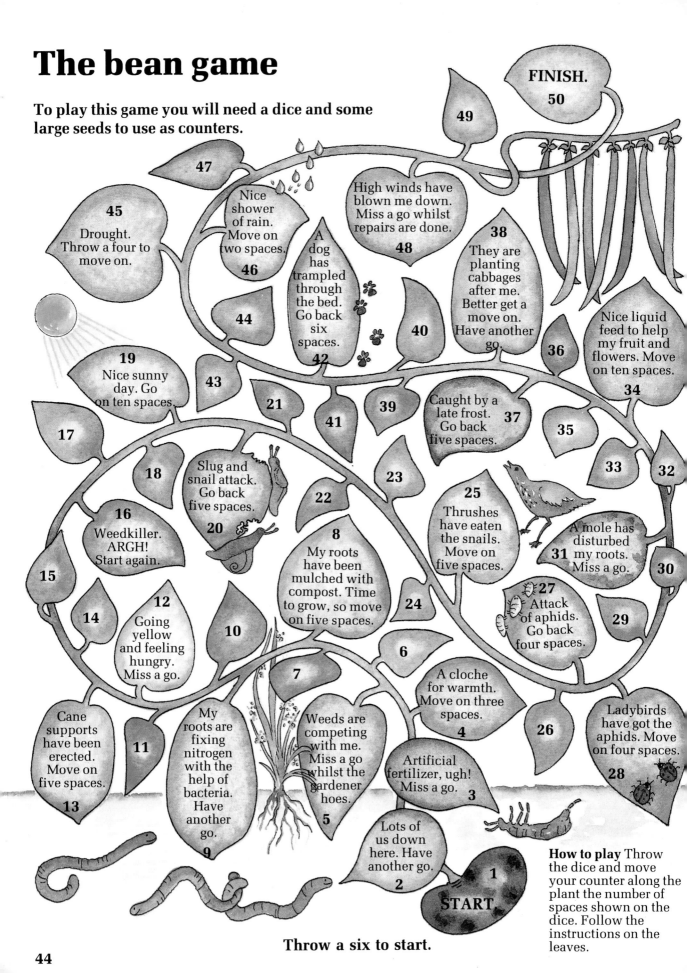

FINISH.
50

49

47

45 Drought. Throw a four to move on.

46 Nice shower of rain. Move on two spaces.

High winds have blown me down. Miss a go whilst repairs are done. **48**

42 A dog has trampled through the bed. Go back six spaces.

38 They are planting cabbages after me. Better get a move on. Have another go.

44

40

36

Nice liquid feed to help my fruit and flowers. Move on ten spaces. **34**

19 Nice sunny day. Go on ten spaces.

43

21

39

41

Caught by a late frost. Go back five spaces. **37**

35

17

33

32

18

20 Slug and snail attack. Go back five spaces.

22

23

25 Thrushes have eaten the snails. Move on five spaces.

31 A mole has disturbed my roots. Miss a go.

30

16 Weedkiller. ARGH! Start again.

27 Attack of aphids. Go back four spaces.

29

15

8 My roots have been mulched with compost. Time to grow, so move on five spaces.

24

26

12 Going yellow and feeling hungry. Miss a go.

14

10

6

A cloche for warmth. Move on three spaces. **4**

Ladybirds have got the aphids. Move on four spaces. **28**

13 Cane supports have been erected. Move on five spaces.

11

7

9 My roots are fixing nitrogen with the help of bacteria. Have another go.

5 Weeds are competing with me. Miss a go whilst the gardener hoes.

3 Artificial fertilizer, ugh! Miss a go.

2 Lots of us down here. Have another go.

1 **START.**

How to play Throw the dice and move your counter along the plant the number of spaces shown on the dice. Follow the instructions on the leaves.

Throw a six to start.

Ladybird answers

4 Anything that is or was once alive.

5 Smelling the soil can tell you whether it is healthy or whether it contains too much water.

6 Organic matter.

7 The worm.

8 There are more bacteria in a teaspoon of soil than there are people on this planet – over five billion!

9 No, only the half with the saddle will survive.

10–11 Chicken and rabbit manures.

12–13 The soil life.

14 A green manure is a plant that is grown and dug back into the soil to feed it.

15 Hoof and horn gives nitrogen, which helps leaves to grow. Bone meal gives phosphate, which helps roots to grow.

16 The advantage of a bed is that once it has been made it does not need to be dug again. This is because there is no need to walk on it, as all the plants can be reached from the path.

17 Pricking out means transferring seedlings to a tray of new compost and spacing them more widely to give them room to grow.

18 Plants are covered with a cloche to keep them warm.

19 Harden off a cutting by putting it outside in its pot for a few hours each day. This will get it used to the outside world before it is planted out.

20 A runner is a shoot that has baby plants along its length.

21 A cutting is a piece of plant, usually a shoot, that has been cut off in order to make it grow roots and become a new plant.

22 Potatoes, carrots, cabbages, and peas.

23 A potato is a swollen stem that stores the potato plant's food underground. It is called a tuber.

24 The legume family.

25 The female flowers have small fruit swellings behind them.

26–7 The boys are pruning in the summer rather than in the autumn, and they are not cutting the old wood close to the ground.

28–9 Chive.

30–1 An annual plant flowers and dies in one year, whilst a biennial plant takes two years to flower and then dies.

32 Plants have flowers to produce seeds, which make new plants.

33 You should not pick wild flowers because this will stop them from producing seeds and making new plants. If not enough new plants are made, then the flowers will gradually disappear altogether and useful wildlife will no longer be attracted.

34–5 All plants need light to grow, so if you do not give them any (by covering the soil) then they will die.

36 Potatoes are poisonous when they are green.

37 An insectivorous bird is one which eats insects.

38 To hibernate means to go to sleep for the winter. Animals such as hedgehogs do this to help them to survive the cold.

39 A marginal plant is one that grows in the shallow parts of a pond.

40–1 No, only hover-fly larvae eat aphids. The adults drink nectar from flowers.

42–3 A predator eats the whole pest in one go, whilst a parasite makes its home on or inside the pest and slowly eats it to live.

Glossary

This list gives the meanings of some of the more difficult gardening and scientific terms used in the book.

? **Can you identify the pictures?** Each one illustrates one of the words described here. (The answers are at the end of the glossary.)

Acid: substances like vinegar and lemon juice are acids. Acids are the opposite of alkalis.

Alkali: substances like bicarbonate of soda are alkalis. Alkalis are the opposite of acids, e.g. if bicarbonate of soda is added carefully to lemon juice, then the lemon juice will lose its tang. This is because the alkali has neutralized (balanced out) the acid.

Annual: the seed of an annual grows into a plant which flowers, seeds, and dies in one year.

Bacteria: very small life forms that consist of one cell. They cannot be seen without a strong microscope.

Barrier: a material that is put on or around plants to stop pests from getting to them.

Bed: an area of soil, used for growing plants, which can be reached from the path and need not be walked upon.

Biennial: the seed of a biennial grows into a plant which takes two years to flower, seed, and die.

Carbon dioxide: a gas that humans breathe out and plants take in to make sugar.

Chemical fertilizer: a plant food made by man that does not feed the life in the soil.

Chemical spray: a poisonous spray made by man that is used to kill pests or weeds.

Compacted soil: soil that has had the important air spaces squashed out of it.

Companion planting: planting together different plants that can help each other to grow.

Compost: a substance made of rotted materials. Compost feeds the soil and helps to build soil crumbs. It also helps to cure many soil problems.

Crop rotation: growing different families of vegetables in separate plots and moving them to a different place each year. This helps to prevent pests and diseases, and it also keeps the soil in good health.

Cutting: a piece of plant (usually a shoot) that has been cut off in order to make it grow roots and become a new plant. Softwood cuttings are taken in the summer from soft growth. Hardwood cuttings are taken in the winter from hard woody shoots.

Division: splitting a plant in half in order to make two new plants.

Dormancy: a period of time when a plant stops growing and has a rest. Seeds sometimes become dormant in the winter so that they can survive the cold.

Fungi: a group of simple life forms that are not green like plants, e.g. mushrooms. Many fungi live as 'threads' beneath the soil and help to make compost.

Germination: the moment when the first root pushes out of the seed.

Green manure: a plant that is grown to be dug back into the soil to feed it.

Hardening off: getting plants used to the outside world after they have been started off in a warm place inside. This is normally done by putting them outside in their pots for a few hours each day.

Hardy plant: a plant that can survive outside all the year round.

Hibernation: a long period of special sleep in the winter which helps certain animals, such as hedgehogs, to survive the cold.

Humus: a black, jelly-like substance that helps to hold the soil crumbs together. It is made from organic matter by the soil life.

Insectivore: a creature which eats insects.

Larva: a type of grub. This is the first stage in an insect's development, and an insect larva looks very different from the adult insect into which it finally changes, e.g. a caterpillar (the larva) looks nothing like a butterfly (the adult).

Layering: a way of helping roots to grow on a plant stem whilst it is still joined to the mother plant.

Leaf mould: leaves that have rotted down.

Legume: a plant that makes food from the nitrogen in the air.

Lime: a plant food and soil improver made of chalk. It feeds the soil and the plants, and it also makes clay soil less sticky.

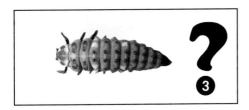

Marginal plant: a plant that grows in the shallow parts of a pond.

Minerals: ground-up rocks which make up part of the soil. Some minerals feed the plants.

Mulch: a covering that is spread over the soil, e.g. grass mowings, newspaper.

Nectar: a food for insects, which is made by flowers.

Neutral: substances that are neither too acid nor too alkaline are neutral. The soil life and most plants prefer neutral soil.

Nitrogen: a gas in the air, which can be made into plant food.

Nutrients: plant foods.

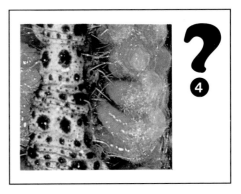

Organic: something that is or was once alive. Organic gardeners work with nature in the garden and recycle all that they can to prevent waste.

Organic fertilizer: a plant food made from dead plants or animals, e.g. bone meal, seaweed meal. It is not bulky and does not build up the soil like compost does.

Organic matter: anything that is or was once alive.

Oxygen: the gas that animals need in order to breathe. Plants can make oxygen in sunlight.

Parasite: an animal or plant that lives in or on, and feeds off, another.

Perennial: a plant with a life cycle of three years or more. Herbaceous perennials die back to ground level each winter, whilst woody perennials leave tough woody stems above the ground.

Pest: an animal or plant that attacks and/or eats plants.

Phosphate: a plant food that helps roots to grow.

Photosynthesis: the process that plants use to make sugar and oxygen from carbon dioxide, water, and sunlight.

Pinching out: nipping out the top of a plant to make it bushy.

Potash: a plant food that helps flowers and fruits to grow.

Predator: an animal that feeds on other animals but is not a parasite.

Pricking out: transferring seedlings to a tray of new compost and spacing them more widely. This gives them more food and more room to grow.

Pruning: cutting unwanted parts off a plant.

Pupa: a stage between the larva and the adult insect. The pupa looks as if it is asleep, but many changes are happening inside it.

Runner: a shoot that has baby plants along its length.

Seed drill: a groove made in the soil in which to plant seeds.

Soil life: creatures living in the soil.

Starch: a substance made from lots of sugars joined together. Bread and potatoes are full of starch. If you chew a piece of bread for a long time, then you can break down the starch and begin to taste the sugar from which it is made.

Subsoil: the layer of soil beneath the topsoil, which has less food and life in it.

Sugar: a food made by plants.

Topsoil: the top layer of soil, which is full of soil life and plant food.

Trace elements: plant foods that are needed only in very small amounts.

Weed: a plant growing in the wrong place.

Worm-cast: worms eat soil and organic matter, and they pass out perfectly formed soil crumbs which are full of food for other soil creatures to live on and in. Worm-casts make up a large part of good soil.

Answers: ❶ annual (poached egg plant) ❷ green manure (clover) ❸ larva (ladybird) ❹ parasite (parasitic wasp) ❺ seed drill.

Index